God's Optimism

Yehoshua November

Winner of the 2010 Main Street Rag Poetry Book Award

MAIN STREET RAG PUBLISHING COMPANY
CHARLOTTE, NORTH CAROLINA

Copyright © 2010 Yehoshua November

Cover artwork by Yehoshua November with adjustments by
M. Scott Douglass
Author photo by: Michael Livshin

Library of Congress Control Number: 2010938519

ISBN: 978-1-59948-264-4

Produced in the United States of America

Main Street Rag
PO Box 690100
Charlotte, NC 28227
www.MainStreetRag.com

Acknowledgments

Many thanks to the publications in which versions of the following poems have appeared:

The Adirondack Review: "Clock Factory Near the River"
The Arava Review: "The Unvisited Lanes"
Audience Review: "A Jewish Poet" and "Upstairs the Eulogy, Downstairs the Rummage Sale"
B'Or Hatorah: "God's Optimism"
European Judaism (London): "Already I Feel Like an Old Man," "Walking"
The Forward: "The Yeshiva Fades From Recollection," "The Meditation of Travel"
I Just Hope It's Lethal (a Houghton Mifflin poetry anthology): "Brotherhood," "How a Place Becomes Holy"
Margie: The American Journal of Poetry: "The Eternal Communists"
Midstream: "Before I Took Up This Journey," "Climbing"
New Vilna Review: "We Go to Work for Unsettled Sums," "Baal Teshuvas at the Mikvah," "This Morning, I Recalled Our Belated Honeymoon," "Upstairs the Eulogy, Downstairs the Rummage Sale"
New Works Review: "A Religion of Tests," "God's Optimism," "Harpo," "The Frierdiker Rebbe"
Prairie Schooner: "Upstairs the Eulogy, Downstairs the Rummage Sale," "Professor," "A Jewish Poet," "Shadows," "The One Who Has Left You," "The First Time," and "The Purpose of This World" (This group of poems was selected as the winner of *Prairie Schooner*'s Bernice Slote Award, and "Upstairs the Eulogy, Downstairs the Rummage Sale" was nominated for a Pushcart Prize)
Provincetown Arts: "Tennis"
The Sun: "Cleaning Out Zaide's Apartment"
The Writers' Café: "The Arizal's Mikvah," "Partners in Creation," "In the Unseeable World"
Zeek: A Jewish Journal of Thought and Culture: "Tangerine"

For my wife, Ahuva Rachel (Amy)

In memory of my grandparents:
  Louis Baer A"H
  Sidney and Ida November A"H

Contents

Foreword ix

We Go to Work for Unsettled Sums 1
Cleaning Out Zaide's Apartment. 2
Professor 3
The One Who Has Left You 4
Walking 5
Yaakov and Rachel 6
Baal Teshuvas at the Mikvah 8
Tennis 10
Anything Infinite Must Be Unknown 11
After Our Wedding 12
The Yeshiva Fades From Recollection 14
A Religion of Tests 15
Art 18
Even When I Was Young 19
Please 20
Tangerine 21
Gift 22
Brotherhood 23
How a Place Becomes Holy 25
Billboards 26
Night 29
The Meditation of Travel 30
Eternal Communists 31

Already I Feel Like an Old Man 32
Climbing. 34
When a Man Leaves His Wife. 35
Descent .36
Mincha .37
The Unvisited Lanes 38
Harpo. .39
God's Optimism 40
My Sweet Bride 41
Clock Factory Near the River 42
In the Unseeable World 43
Synchronicity 44
The Frierdiker Rebbe 46
This Morning, I Recalled Our Belated Honeymoon . .48
Partners in Creation 51
The Arizal's Mikvah. 52
The First Time. 53
Every Friday Night 54
Shadows 55
A Jewish Poet 57
The Purpose of This World 58
Upstairs the Eulogy, Downstairs the Rummage Sale . .59
Before I Took Up This Journey 61
Glossary
Special Thanks

Foreword

I remember the first time I met Yehoshua November, many long years ago in an introductory poetry class. I went around the room asking each student an ice-breaking question that felt, even then, a bit perfunctory: why did they write poetry? When we came to Josh (that's what we called him then), he said, "I want to restore the sanctity to language."

The class was startled. I was stunned, and never forgot it, partly because over the years I have watched him wrestle to do just that. Yehoshua went on to finish his undergraduate and advanced degrees, become a teacher, marry and raise a family. But he has never stopped writing poetry and he has never stopped trying to restore an essential sanctity to language. I feel him grappling with the spiritual in every poem—as Jacob said when he wrestled all night, "I will not let Thee go except Thou bless me." Even when the poem is about apparently mundane subjects—tennis, billboards, Harpo Marx, a tangerine—this tension between the daily and the sacred hums just under its skin.

Reading this glorious book of poems, one of the finest I have read in decades, part of me thinks, well of course God is an optimist if He's still got someone like Yehoshua November on his side. Sanctified but never sanctimonious, many of the poems in *God's Optimism* dive into the subjects of desire, longing, passion. "When I was a student/ love treated me like a road," November writes in "The One Who Has Left You." He goes on: "because you will find yourself/ sitting alone in a movie house,/ watching the film you planned to see together./ And the man on the screen/ will have dark hair and a distant face/ but the woman will have the eyes/ of the one who has left you." —But there is no telling when there will be a reconciliation: "Then one day the radio returns/ in the middle of the same song,/ like a man waking to finish the sentence/ he began before his coma./ And the lovers, too,/ take up each others' bodies once again,/ but now they are old/ and the love making is slow and awkward, like the first time."

Many of the best poems here are love poems for his own wife, recalling "when, despite the school of nervous fish/ that swam through my heart,/ my hand found yours/ for the first time." These are not ordinary love poems, bound up in them are contradictions, gratitude, and a sense of having found the bershert, or fated one: "if you must rouse me,/ please, my wife,/ do not even place your small hand/ on my shoulders,/ but whisper my name,/ remind me that I am such and such a man/ and you are the dark-haired daughter of so and so,/ chosen for me/ before I took up this journey."

No book of poems can be truly great which does not stretch its attention and compassion toward the larger world. November does this again and again. He goes back in time to the notes his grandmother wrote his grandfather, "*Hard boiled eggs on the stove. I believe in you.*" With great gentleness he reaches for the gifts of his ancestors, "we push our fingers to the back/ of our sock drawers/ and bring the ancient bow ties to the lamplight." Or further, to the last century, the Frierdiker Rebbe cast out of Russia, "*The soul is never in exile.*" He reaches outward as well, to "the nearly naked supermodel/ advertising a watch" on a billboard, whose third marriage is falling apart. He remembers the traveler, "in a foreign province," and his lonely meditations: "not unlike carrying a cello/ through a winter night,/ the dark wood rotting/ in the snow." He writes with compassion about the suicide's father; about "The dark children swimming in the ocean/ off a small town in Chile/…And what about God? If God is infinite, we cannot explain/ the sadness of the world/ without drowning Him."

To read *God's Optimism* is to remember what poetry is meant to be: musical, tender, philosophical, generous-hearted. When I read November's poetry I am ashamed ever to have called myself a poet, for I know I am in the presence of a young master—as honest and witty as Kafka, as visionary as Doestoevski, but with a voice and presence all his own. This book is an astonishing debut. While rooted deeply in its Jewishness, it speaks to people of all faiths, and of no faith. The first person (among many) to whom I will gift this book is a lay Catholic priest, for I know it will speak to him. There is nothing holier-than-thou in November's sanctity of language. It is filled with contradictions and dualities, as many of the poems' titles suggest, "Anything Infinite Must Be Unknown," "Upstairs the Eulogy, Downstairs the Rummage Sale." I will gladly give the book to the local Chassidic rabbi's wife, or to my wildest, most rebellious student with pink and blue hair.

November's work has been published in the most prestigious literary magazines, has won awards, been anthologized, and is destined to reach an ever-widening audience. His voice is magically lyrical, "and every voice could be the one/ that dissolves in the forest/ or the song that holds/ the necklace of the lake." More than that, it shows wisdom far beyond his years, for November is still a young poet, and one could hardly expect such depths from a writer three times his age. I'll end by quoting one of my favorite poems, "Tennis," in full:

> One evening you will walk past a park
> between two fading apartment buildings,
> and see men playing tennis in white garments,
> and long to slip out of your life,
> to be buried in the white robe with no pockets,
> and float like the ball
> between two rivals, two great friends,
> this world and the next.

What you hold in your hands, reader, is not just a book of poems, but a treasure.

Liz Rosenberg,
July 2010

We Go To Work For Unsettled Sums

It's amazing the gifts we are given,
and still how often we go to the usurer,
how long it takes to find good work,
only to remain with the same old itch,
pushing us to the same places we've looked,
not knowing if the butcher's thumb
leans on the scale.
And every hoofbeat could have us on the floor,
the horse tired of reciting master,
and every voice could be the one
that dissolves in the forest
or the song that holds
the necklace of the lake.

Cleaning Out Zaide's Apartment
For My Grandparents

His scent still lingered in the black heat
of his darkroom, where he spent decades
developing his meticulous world
of insects and flowers.
Boxes of slides
lay piled on top of one another.
Holding one to the lamplight,
I entered a different universe,
where moths silently cling to the stems
of roses.

In the bedroom
we found tie clips in the shape of airplanes
and then the slender, fragile model planes
he had built from scratch and hand painted
bright blue with yellow emblems on the wings.

And in every drawer,
countless notes she had written to him.
He must have saved them all,
each one wedding the mundane to a private world
only the lovers themselves could know:
Hard boiled eggs on the stove. I believe in you.

Professor

So we enter the library once more
in search of the *self*,
as though it were not a word made up in the university,
where students in jeans and professors in jackets and scarves
long for eternal truths
and to be published,
to be read by other professors as they slip off
their coats and hang them on the backs of their office chairs
and dip into the years of lonely research
and the otherness of bus rides home.

Professor, who is it that owns truth,
where is the pool that reflects our grieving faces?
Did you have to give the lecture
on the imminent failure of marriage?

Once when we met in your office
and you turned to your shelf to draw down a book
that had changed your life,
while your back was toward me,
I concentrated all my energy on whispering *Hashem's* name,
all irony faded
and angels were swimming from your lamp.

The One Who Has Left You

When I was a student
love treated me like a road
Jewish girls would travel down
each her own distance

until summer came and she would go to camp
and by the lake give her heart
to one of the older boys,
who worked in the kitchen
and smoked behind the sports shack
on the Sabbath.

And I learned never to make predictions
about a love you are a part of
because you will find yourself
sitting alone in a movie house,
watching the film you planned to see together.

And the man on the screen
will have dark hair and a distant face
but the woman will have the eyes
of the one who has left you.

Walking

The Rabbis say that every step a Jew walks
in the direction of the *shul*
is a step toward happiness in the world to come,
and if it's snowing, or very late, or very early,
each step counts as two.

And if he brings his son with him,
he is rewarded for the steps of the generations
that follow, even if their *shuls*
are miles and centuries
from the road where he and his son walked.

And although he is punished for the things he does
when he finds himself in her room,
sliding off his shoes,
a Jew walking toward another woman's love
is not punished for each step it takes to get there.

This is the mercy of God,
who believes we can do otherwise
until the very moment we sin.
This is the will man has been given,
to bring great sadness into the world.

Yaakov and Rachel
(a late birthday poem)

The first time he saw her,
Yaakov rolled a great rock from the mouth
of the well, where Rachel's sheep
stood in their coats,
dreaming of water.
And knowing they would someday wed,
and that God had led him directly to her,
with tears in his eyes,
Yaakov bent forward to kiss Rachel.

One night, when we had known each other
for only a month or two—
when the suggestion of spending an evening together
would have met, at best,
with a flattered no thank you—
I found myself alone with you,
by the garbage cans
behind the kosher cafeteria.
Overcome by your dark beauty,
I almost leaned in to kiss you,
but I could not budge the weight of my fear.

A few years later,
beneath our wedding canopy,
the rabbi announced,
*The bride's middle name is Rachel and her first name is Ahuva,
which means love.*

The groom's middle name is Yaakov.
This means, if added up, that Yaakov loves Rachel.

I am sorry that, this year, I did not
bring you a poem on your birthday,
and that I am often too lost
in another world to be helpful.
Perhaps it is because these are not our first names
that I have not made the story of our love
more obvious.

Tonight, almost six years into our marriage,
feeling strange traveling without you,
as I eat the sandwiches you prepared for my trip,
I read the famous verse once more:
And Yaakov kissed Rachel and he cried.

And in *Rashi's* commentary
at the bottom of the page,
Yaakov's tears are explained:

For, unlike his forefathers,
who had gathered bracelets and rings for their brides,
Yaakov stood empty-handed before the woman
to whom he owed his life.

Baal Teshuvas at the Mikvah

Sometimes you see them
in the dressing area
of the ritual bath,
young bearded men unbuttoning
their white shirts,
slipping out of their black trousers,
until, standing entirely naked,
they are betrayed by the tattoos
of their past life:
a ring of fire climbing up a leg,
an eagle whose feathery wing span
spreads the width of the chest,
or worse, the scripted name of a woman
other than one's wife.

Then, holding only a towel,
they begin, once more, the walk
past the others in the dressing room:
the rabbi they will soon sit before
in Talmud class,
men with the last names
of the first Chasidic families,
almost everyone,
devout since birth.

And with each step,
they curse the poverty
that keeps the dark ink
etched in their skin,

until, finally, they descend the stairs
of the purifying water
and, beneath the translucent liquid,
appear once again
like the next man,

who, in all his days,
has probably never made a sacrifice
as endearing to God.

Tennis

One evening you will walk past a park
between two fading apartment buildings,
and see men playing tennis in white garments,
and long to slip out of your life,
to be buried in the white robe with no pockets,
and float like the ball
between two rivals, two great friends,
this world and the next.

Anything Infinite Must Be Unknown

The dark children swimming in the ocean
off a small town in Chile
will live forever
because you have never been there
and will never learn their names.

All that we do not know remains
forever. Everything we touch or comprehend
in this world
is marked for death.

And what about God?
If God is infinite, we cannot explain
the sadness of the world
without drowning Him.

After Our Wedding

When you forgot the address of our hotel
in your suitcase,
the driver had to pull over
in front of a restaurant.

Men and women dining beneath the August sun
looked up from their salads
to clap for you,
a young, slender woman
in a wedding dress and tiara,
retrieving a slip of paper
from the trunk of a cab
in the middle of the street.

And since that day,
many of the guests at our wedding have divorced
or are gone,
and the restaurant has closed
to become a tattoo parlor.
And we have misplaced and found
many more papers,
but no one was clapping.

And the motion of the lives around us
has been like a great bus
slowly turning onto a crowded street.
And some of the passengers
have fallen asleep in their seats,

while others anxiously search
their jacket pockets
for the notes that might wed
their ordinary lives
to something lofty and astonishing.

The Yeshiva Fades From Recollection

The yeshiva fades from recollection
and in the spaces of memory where voices are stored,
the rabbis of my youth chant questions and answers,
as they swim through the Talmud.
And when I have fallen—
there is the image of the head rabbi,
his disciples assimilated in a circle of dance,
until he, too, slowly and deliberately
asserts his inheritance,
closes his eyes, gives his arms to the air,
and movement by movement
departs and returns to this world.

And what is it that I have ignored,
that has brought me here,
only to watch the others dance?

A Religion of Tests

I

How beautiful, I said,
when I noticed the plaque above two of the synagogue's
bookshelves:

*This collection of the Rebbe's teachings
donated so that the soul of the departed little girl___
daughter of Rabbi___ will merit an elevation.*

And I imagined the Rebbe's thoughts curling upwards
through the minds of young men
who had drawn books from these shelves
on Friday evenings,
as the Sabbath descended,

while, in the upper realms, the little girl
experienced one weightless ascent after another,
traveling ever deeper into the region of secrets,
only a bodiless soul can know.

But then I thought,
God should not let it happen,
and I imagined losing my own eldest daughter,
and a sharp pain found my stomach,
as I pictured her name and mine
carved plainly above the shelves.

II

God, You have made it clear that this is a religion of tests,
but in the books of mysticism
You have also whispered that all the while
You hide just behind the wall,
waiting for us to pass.

And in the pages of *Chasidus*,
You have lectured that even Your concealment
is a paradox.
The soul is exiled from the world
of unity above,
sentenced to life in a heavy and strange body,
only so that, by its own strength,
in the darkness,
the soul might reveal You
in this lower world as well.

Still, as we lift our faces from our books
and walk out the synagogue's heavy glass doors,
we wonder if You have not hidden
Yourself too well.

And, on more difficult days,
some of us conclude that our tests are not
passable, after all.

III

Yet, once, at the Sabbath afternoon services,
I saw a man praying.
His hair was combed perfectly,
but his heart was broken.
A month earlier his son had jumped
from the city's tallest building.

I saw him rocking back and forth in prayer
like a flame.
The synagogue's lights reflected off his forehead,
and everyone who was there knew
he was very close to God.

Art

Art is like the sleep
a mourner resorts to
on the first night without his beloved.

In the morning he must come back to the world
to empty the closet of her blouses and belts
and give them to strangers.

Even When I Was Young

Some Jews say
that a number of possible soul mates
await us in this world,
and depending on which way we turn,
we will meet one of the chosen.

When I was a student, my family lived
in many cities.
And in each city there was at least one girl
with long, dark eyelashes
or a tired voice that, over the phone,
seemed to hold the honey
of my redemption.

For, even then,
even as a boy,
I awaited your earth-like song,
the song that would send
the rest of the women
to redeem the destinies
of other strangers.

Please

Do not bring us your stories
of sunlight shooting across
a canvas
of sparrows sleeping on dusty windowsills
of a perfumed young woman in a dim flat, waiting
for the town magician,
of boys studying under the same rebbe
until they are men,
of men standing on lonely bridges
beneath the magnificent sky,
where the apparitions of their dead wives
appear to them.
Please, we cannot believe in anything.

Tangerine
For My Grandmother

I know you only as a small boy knows an old woman
peeling a tangerine for his small mouth
and from the inscription in the Yevtushenko book
you gave my father when he was a boy:
May you never be afraid of your Russian sensitivity.

But as I read your notebooks
I see that we share the same fear of science,
and a distrust for all the gifts we have not earned.

And on the Sabbath before my wedding–
a day after my father and I had visited the cemetery
to invite you and Zaide to the ceremony–
a stranger in a *shul* I had never been to
asked me my name and if I knew you.

Ma Shissel,
I know you are watching over me,
peeling the hardships from my days,
allowing me to live as a boy
who has never put the hard skin of the world
to his lips.

Gift

We find odd jobs
to keep us abreast of our sorrows.
We recall our sad lives on long train rides
or buses that carry us across minor towns.
In the hallways of strange buildings
we try to look more at others' faces,
to remember our mother's singing voice.
And limping home after long days
of ignoring our true work,
we are reminded of the bow tie
our grandfathers wore the first time
they saw our grandmothers.
And finally in our bedrooms,
we push our fingers to the back
of our sock drawers
and bring the ancient bow ties to the lamplight.

Brotherhood

The first boy to fall in
love with my then future wife
was a second grader
with wild curly hair
and sharp eyes,
the class clown,
Maurice,

who accidentally signed
an anonymous love letter
he sent her in the mail,

who, in the shadows
of the school coatroom,
uncloaked his sex
and held it before her eyes
like a rare, tropical fish
that would surely
die if left
too long in the open air.

Maurice,
I am told that,
a few years later,
they put you in an institution.

And I imagine that
as you watched your father and mother's car
fade behind a row of trees
and turned your face
back to the asylum doors,

hundreds of miles away,
a heaviness found my heart.

How a Place Becomes Holy

Sometimes a man
will start crying in the middle of the street,
without knowing why or for whom.
It is as though someone else is standing there,
holding his briefcase, wearing his coat.

And from beneath the rust of years,
come to his tongue the words of his childhood:
"I'm sorry," and "God," and "Do not be far from me."

And just as suddenly the tears are gone,
and the man walks back into his life,
and the place where he cried becomes holy.

Billboards

Each weeknight,
after teaching at an evening college,
I begin the drive back to my wife and children,
merging onto the ramp
beneath the nearly naked supermodel
advertising a watch,

just one billboard after the mediation services ad,
which asks, DIVORCING?
in shining purple letters three times a man's height,
and then goes on,
WE CAN HELP, in letters a bit smaller.

Feeling lonely one night on that road,
in the space between the two signs,
I called my friend
under the pretense of adding another line
to our running joke
about the man his sister had married.

But after a long, laugh-less pause,
I learned that she,
along with her two children,
had moved back to her old bedroom
in her parents' house,
down the hall from
another divorced sibling.

And when I finally arrived home that night,
my wife, excited to see me,
got off the phone
with her divorced college friend,
who said she knew a number
of great discussion groups
for my wife's recently divorced cousin.

But how, to begin with,
do two people never related by blood
unpack everything they have separately collected
into shared rooms?

And then, with what strength do they repack
and empty the rooms they have filled?

What is the name of the force
that finally carries each one alone
through the hallway
and into the open evening?

On my drive home tonight,
I learn over the radio
that the model has just separated from her third husband.

But in the billboard,
she continues to look out at the world
with her careless smile,
as cars drift into the darkness of the interstate.

Night

In the darkness of his dormitory,
a student of German poetry
will wake to the sound of a rushing fountain
and a light gleaming
beneath his bathroom door,
and, perceiving the outline of his roommate
asleep beneath his pallid quilt,
rise from his bed
to learn the source of the water and the light,
turn the handle of the weightless creaking door
and behold, of course, Goethe
scrubbing his undergarments in the sink.
Until, the eternally private poet
lifts his gray head
to the bathroom mirror
to meet the student's reflection
with the eyes of the Black Forest.

The Meditation of Travel

To warm ourselves before a stove
in a foreign province,
to rise early,
the wayfarer's prayer
on our tongues,
to watch fish blaze through shallow streams
and think of home,
to shift our load from one shoulder to the next
and be reminded of the faces
of lovers that failed us
ages ago.
All these form the meditation of travel,
all these are not unlike carrying a cello
through a winter night,
the dark wood rotting
in the snow.

The Eternal Communists

The eternal communists
with their short pointy beards
and serious faces
are protesting
in the marble lobby
of the free world.
Among them are some men
with longer beards–
university professors.
From their mouths bloom eloquent arguments
about oppression and poverty.
They speak as though they would tenderly give
half their beds to the refugees,
though they can't even live
with the women they love,
and they don't know
the history of the war
or that the refugees have explosives
hidden in the fillings of their teeth.

Already I Feel Like an Old Man

"Married at twenty-two?" they ask,
"But that's so young."

Yet, in the gray *shtetels* of Russia,
less than a century ago,
a violin mender's apprentice
might marry at seventeen.
His bride, the bean merchant's daughter,
only fifteen.
Both quite certain of their purpose:

He, returning home each evening
with a loaf of dark bread in his fist,
speaking of the rain.
She, cooking lentil soup in winter.

This is our lineage.

Besides, I could not imagine
being alone in that way again,
and what would the Sabbath be
without you?

Already I feel like an old man.

All those mornings I awoke
like a traveler
in a rented room, who,
in the darkness,
mistakes the blankets and sheets
for his own
and wonders who moved the lamp
to the other side of the bed.

Climbing

This morning,
in the small basement *shul*,
amidst several Chasidic students lost in prayer,
I looked up from my *siddur*
to see a man in worker's clothes climb a ladder
and enter through an open ceiling panel.
And I thought, Oh yes,
he is just another one
like all of us
trying desperately to ascend,
but knowing full well he must come back down
to perform the work of this earth.

When A Man Leaves His Wife

In a suitcase he carries all the things he has saved
in the course of his days,
and in his chest he carries a sadness
he has always known.

And as he drives through the streets
he thinks, *I will keep driving
until I reach the road
that leads out of my life with her,*

because he does not remember
that the loneliness he is carrying
belongs to her.

Descent

This morning,
as snow descended weightlessly
in the synagogue window,
I was overtaken by the secret
of why You exile a soul from the realm of oneness
to carry a dark trunk, alone,
through the unending streets of this world.
And I understood fully
the teaching that an hour given to You
in this earthly life
is greater than all the radiance of the next one.
But soon, a fog-like forgetfulness
usurped the moment's clarity.
Life's heaviness returned.

Mincha

In the winter,
when the onset of twilight coincided
with our ten minute break from poetry workshop,
I would rise from the table
where I had sat in silence
as students read lines on the mercilessness
of God,
husbands sitting next to voluptuous strangers
on train rides,
and the lack of spiritual urgency
demonstrated by businessmen—

and with a small *siddur*
hidden in my pocket,
descend the stairwell,
walk through a long white hallway of offices
where secretaries stared into the glow
of computer screens
and spoke of cities without snow,

past the classroom
where a professor of interior design
discussed curtains with lingering students,

until I reached the small alcove by the large window,
tied the belt that divides
the upper body from the lower organs
around my waist,
and, in the last moments of daylight,
turned east to pray.

The Unvisited Lanes

A groomer of wigs knows certain tricks.
A laundress knows of a lake that washes blood
from a prayer shawl.
A blind man
can remember precisely
the roads of his boyhood, the tilted face
of the last girl he saw leaning toward him.

What have you learned
between music and the gray winter rain?

In the unvisited lanes so many are waiting.

Harpo

Inimitable and wordless
master of improvisation,
with your baggy trench coat
of useless goods
and your wild curly blond wig,
which comedian,
even in his most opulent fantasy,
could hope to contrive the lines that formed
your unusually large smile?

And who else could roll up his pant legs
to wash his feet and dance
in a burly street vender's lemonade tank?

And who would have known
that, after performances,
the most lighthearted of five brothers
would race to his wife and children,
instead of card games and wild women?

And should that really surprise us
when we recall how,
sometimes,
you put down your simple horn,
and turned, adeptly, heartbreakingly,
to your harp?

God's Optimism
For Norman Maranz

Because the nature of a stone
is not to fly,
it remains in the air only
as long as the thrower's force
acts upon it.

And in the inner Torah
the same is said of this world,
which comes from nothing
and whose nature, therefore,
is not to exist. It remains
only as long as God pushes it into existence.

Think of the optimism of God, then,
how, every second, He recreates our lives–
I who have not served Him honestly,
and you who believe you have never served Him.

My Sweet Bride

Whatever sadness greets us,
whatever sorrows smuggle past our *mezuzah*,
we will always return to that room,
our first moments alone—

when, despite the school of nervous fish
that swam through my heart,
my hand found yours
for the first time.

I heard the song of your bosom
I was born to learn,

felt your fingers
climb the lanes
of my arms,
like humble trains that port
estranged companions
to the villages of their childhood.

We will always return to that moment,
when I sat beside you,
not knowing then
you would be my bride.

Clock Factory Near the River

After a while, a man who works in a clock factory
begins to mistake the constant ticking
for the sound of water
dripping in a deep well
his great-grandfather
once spoke of.
And it is only after he has returned
his apron and tools to his locker,
and come through the heavy doors
into evening,
and walked along the river with the other men,
that time and water are once again
separate things.

In the Unseeable World

Sometimes, when a boy reaches for a ball
in his dream, his sleeping hand
claws through the empty air of this world.
And his brother, sleepless in the next bed, says,
He reaches for nothing,
it is all a dream.

Sometimes, when a man passes the window of a *shul*,
he sees another man swaying
and stretching his arms heavenward,

and in the unseeable world, *Hashem's*
long arms reach through the eternal
water and the firmament
and His hands cleave
to the hands of the man who is praying.

And the man passing by says,
Oh, why does he waste his energy,
what does he hope to touch?

Synchronicity

Several Chasidim walk through a grassy cemetery
in search of their teacher's grave.
And though they have passed it several times
in the last half hour,
they cannot find his headstone,

where two portly Belarusian men,
with failing vision,
argue and weep before the plot
they mistake for their mother's,

who died four years ago, in her apartment,
falling from her chair—
where she sat
after an afternoon at the market—
to the kitchen floor,

while the fish she had just bought
flopped from her old wooden cutting board,
then to the counter,
then to her warm Belarusian breast,
dying there.
Both lying peacefully beneath the evening
that descended through her
kitchen window.

But suddenly, the tallest Chasid is perplexed,
as he remembers lowering the coffin near a tree
with branches not unlike the ones
on which the Belarusians
have hung their scarves.
Only, in memory,
the tree was not that tall,
so he does not mention it to his friends.

And across the street,
fourth row, second plot,
before a scarf-less tree,
the Belarusians' mother lies unvisited,
except by the shadow
of a government building

wherein the wife of the tallest Chasid—
born in a town separated from the Belarusians'
only by a lake
that has since lost its name—
has just entered the lobby and asked,
in tragic broken English,
Which floor for divorce papers?

The Frierdiker Rebbe

And isn't it amazing
that men walked by you in Latvian hallways,
and had no idea they were passing a man
who knew the day they would die and the women
they would marry,
but also asked simple questions
at information booths, like
How many miles to Nikaloyev?
and *Will I arrive before nightfall?*
until these words too were flooded
with the mysticism of every Russian lake.

And at the station in St. Petersburg,
where your Chasidim had gathered,
risking their lives
to see you one last time,
you turned from the steps of the train
that was to carry you into exile
and proclaimed,
They only have our bodies;
the soul was never separated from God.
The soul is never in exile.

There was even holiness in the rain
that fell on the hats of your followers
as they paced before the river in Rostov,
reciting your discourses by heart,
line by line,

until they would float like boats
into the luminescence of your teachings.

This Morning, I Recalled Our
Belated Honeymoon

On the wallpaper
of the small Parisian hotel room,
aristocratic couples lounged beside
a forest's opening.

From the window,
you could reach out your hand
and feel the bricks of the next building,
stare down into the dark void below.

And do you remember
when the teenager
at the kosher bakery
invited us to his family's Sabbath meal?

That week, we had stood
before the famous goddess with wings
but no head,
looked up in admiration,
wheeling our suitcases
through the triumphal arch.
We had seen our faces reflected in each
of Louis XIV's mirrors, but,

in the end,
sitting in that family's cramped living room,
at the round table with fish and candles,
didn't it burn so clearly
that we were just

two Jews?
And do you remember how,
hoping we were not
a young unmarried couple
traveling together,
the boy's pious father finally whispered to me,
You are brother and sister?

This morning,
I found the portrait
the insistent street artist drew of you
the final evening of our trip.

Do you remember the huge bump
that grew out of his forehead?
His long, gray hair
and oversized coat.
His wolf-like eyes
staring down
at his canvas—

as snow descended
on Montmartre—

and then looking up,
once again,

into your lovely face.

Partners In Creation

Every moment God recreates the world,
whispering over and over again
the ten Divine utterances
that first gave birth to existence,

the way a child's world is renewed
when he comes home from school
and his father and mother
still live in the same house,
and he hears them talking at the kitchen table.

The Arizal's Mikvah

To walk, just before the Sabbath descends,
a borrowed towel over your shoulder,
down the green hill
that leads to the cemetery of Cabalists,
to pass through the narrow lanes between the gravestones
and hesitate by the Arizal's grave,
to sense the souls of his students
hovering over his gravestone,
to know for certain that he too hovers there,
only a little higher,
rocking back and forth, like a flame.
To walk a few yards east
and enter the mouth of the Arizal's cave,
to slowly remove your clothes in the heavy air
and descend into the cold spring,
to leave this world for a moment,
to know one day
all those you have forsaken
will forgive you.

The First Time

Sometimes, in the middle of a journey,
the radio will break,
and the traveler will be left without music
for the rest of his wandering.
He will drive from city to city with the last song he heard.

Sometimes, in the middle of love,
the two parties stop speaking
and it goes on this way for years.
Though they no longer touch,
each one falls asleep to the memory
of the last time they made love.

Then one day the radio returns
in the middle of the same song,
like a man waking to finish the sentence
he began before his coma.

And the lovers, too,
take up each others' bodies once again,
but now they are old
and the love making is slow and awkward,
like the first time.

Every Friday Night

Every Friday night Jewish men walk home from *shul*

and as they pass barber shops
and travel agencies

a Semitic sadness weighs on their shoulders
like a father's coat on a small boy.

And sometimes it's the thought
that God will go on concealing Himself
that casts this grayness
over the Sabbath evening

but more often it's the blond woman
who walks through the mind of every Jewish man,

leading him away from his dark haired wife.

Shadows
For My Wife

You do not remember the first time we met.
It was a crowded night in Jerusalem,
at the bottom of Ben Yehuda Street.

I said to myself,
"Who is this dark girl
with a space between her front teeth?"
But you did not even look at me.

And as you walked away,
the friend who introduced us asked me,
"What do you think?"
I said, "Okay, I guess,"
as I watched you fade up the street
into a crowd of students and soldiers.

I watched you
the way young men watch women
before they have loved them,
and I sent my shadow hungrily after you,
the way some send their shadows
when their bodies
cannot go.

That night,
I walked back to the Old City alone,
through the Jaffa Gate,

past the dark mouth
of the Arab market,
through the lane along David's Fortress.
By the time I reached the yeshiva,
my roommates were sleeping.

Years later,
I sat with my brother at the *Shabbos* table
in a *shul* oceans and wars
away from Jerusalem.
When I looked up,
the dark girl with the space between her teeth.

In this life,
we make many strange deals,
what must one give up
for the return of his shadow?

A Jewish Poet

It is hard to be a Jewish poet.
You cannot say things about God
that will offend the disbelievers.
And you always have to remind someone
it wasn't your people who killed their savior.
And Solomon and David are always laughing
over your shoulder
like a father and son ridiculing the unfavored brother.
And you cannot entice people with the sloping
parts of a woman's body
because you must always remain pure.
And every day you have to ask yourself why you're writing
when there is already the one great book.
It is hard to be a Jewish poet.
You cannot say anything about the disbelievers,
which might offend God.

The Purpose of This World

When some Jews cannot explain the sorrow of their lives
they take a vow of atheism.
Then everywhere they go,
they curse the God they don't believe exists.

But why, why don't they grab Him by the lapels,
pull His formless body down into this lowly world,
and make Him explain.

After all, this is the purpose of creation–
to make this coarse realm a dwelling place for His presence.

Upstairs the Eulogy, Downstairs the Rummage Sale

The beloved Yiddish professor
passed away on the same day
as the synagogue's rummage sale,

and because they could not bear
the coffin up the many steps
that led to the sanctuary,
they left it in the hallway downstairs,

and because I was not one of his students,
and it didn't matter if I heard the eulogy,
they told me to stay downstairs,
to watch over the body and recite Psalms.

And I thought,
this is how it is in the life and death of a righteous man:
upstairs, in the sanctuary, they speak of you in glowing terms,
while down below your body rests beside
old kitchen appliances.

And I recited the Psalms as intently
as I could over a man I had only met once,
and because I knew where he was headed,
and you and I were to wed in a few months,
I asked that he bring with him a prayer for a good marriage.

And this is how it is in the life and death of a righteous man:
strangers pray over the sum of your days,
and strangers ask you to haul their heavy requests
where you cannot even take your body.

Before I Took Up This Journey

Before God opens His fist
to let a soul gently descend into this world,
He whispers a name, an occupation, a future bride:
"So and so the architect will marry so and so the teacher's daughter."
If I lie asleep in my bed–
wherein the Sages say a man's soul goes back,
and he is partly dead–
if you must rouse me,
please, my wife,
do not even place your small hand
on my shoulders,
but whisper my name,
remind me that I am such and such a man
and you are the dark-haired daughter of so and so,
chosen for me
before I took up this journey.

Glossary

The Arizal, Rabbi Isaac Luria, was a 16th century Cabalist. His mikvah, ritual bath, is located in Tsefas, Israel, right next to the cemetery where he and many other noted Cabalists are buried. It is said that one who immerses in these waters is guaranteed to repent before he or she dies.

Baal Teshuva is a Hebrew term which, translated literally, means a master of return or repentance. Today, however, it is more commonly used in reference to a Jew who adopts a life of traditional Judaism, after growing up in a home less committed to traditional Jewish practices.

Chasidus is the literature and philosophy of the Chasidic movement.

The Frierdiker Rebbe was the sixth leader, or Rebbe, of the Chabad-Lubavitch Chasidic dynasty. His 1927 death sentence for spreading Jewish ritual practices in Communist Russia was ultimately commuted to a sentence in exile, from which he was also released just a few days later. He then moved to Latvia and eventually to America.

The Hebrew term *Hashem* literally translates as The Name; it serves as a title by which one can refer to God without mentioning His sacred name.

The Inner Torah refers to the cabalistic or esoteric realm of biblical interpretation, the secrets of the Torah, as opposed to surface-level or non-mystical understanding.

A *mezuzah* is a scroll containing the sacred writings of the Shema prayer; it is placed on the doorpost and is said to offer special protection.

A *Mikvah* is a ritual bath. In many Chasidic communities, men immerse in a mikvah to prepare spiritually for the morning prayer service.

Mincha is the afternoon prayer, which should be prayed before sunset.

Rashi was a fundamental commentator on the Bible and the Talmud. His commentary, written in small scripted letters, appears beneath the original text of most Hebrew Bibles.

A *siddur* is a prayer book.

Yaakov is Hebrew for Jacob. "Yaakov and Rachel" alludes to the biblical love story of Jacob and Rachel. Ultimately, Jacob worked under his father- in- law, Laban, for fourteen toilsome years to gain permission to marry Laban's daughter, Rachel.

Special Thanks

Many thanks to my teachers: Michael Huff, Maria Mazziotti Gillan, Ruth Stone, Joseph Church, Tony Hoagland, and Toi Derricotte. Special thanks to Lynn Emanuel for her helpful comments on the manuscript. Thank you to Rivky Slonim for her important input on these poems and for her constant encouragement. And deepest gratitude to Liz Rosenberg for her invaluable insights on the manuscript and for her support over the years.

Thank you to Rabbi Dick and the faculty at Yeshiva Tiferes Bachurim; thank you to the Slonims for their warmth and guidance; thank you to Miriam Grossman of Touro College for her support; and thank you to the Writing Program and Writers House at Rutgers University.

I am grateful to my parents, Nancy and Stephen November; my brother Baruch; and my sisters Deena and Leora. Thank you to my mother and father in-law, Diane and Jerry Reich, whose tireless efforts to entertain their grandchildren gave me the time to complete this book.

Thank you to my wonderful children. And thank you to my dear wife. You are the inspiration behind many of these poems, and your strength and patience are the foundation of whatever I have achieved.